GOLDEN CHILD

BY DAVID HENRY HWANG

★

★

DRAMATISTS
PLAY SERVICE
INC.

GOLDEN CHILD
Copyright © 1999, David Henry Hwang

All Rights Reserved

SPECIAL NOTE

SPECIAL NOTE ON SONGS AND RECORDINGS

GOLDEN CHILD was produced on Broadway by Benjamin Mordecai, Dori Berinstein, John Kao, Talia Shire Schwartzman and John F. Kennedy Center for the Performing Arts in association with South Coast Repertory and The Joseph Papp Public Theater/New York Shakespeare Festival and American Conservatory Theater, at the Longacre Theatre, in New York City, on April 2, 1998. The Associate Producer was The Singapore Repertory Theater. It was directed by James Lapine; the set design was by Tony Straiges; the costume design was by Martin Pakledinaz; the lighting design was by David J. Lander; the sound design was by Dan Moses Schreier; incidental music was by Lucia Hwong; and the production stage manager was Allison Sommers. The cast was as follows:

ANDREW KWONG/ENG TIENG-BIN	Randall Duk Kim
ENG AHN, daughter of Tieng-Bin and Siu-Young	Julyana Soelistyo
ENG SIU-YOUNG, first wife	Tsai Chin
ENG LUAN, second wife	Kim Miyori
ENG ELING, third wife	Ming-Na Wen
REVEREND BAINES, a missionary	John Horton
SERVANTS/GHOSTS	Julienne Hanzelka Kim, Lisa Li, James Saito

GOLDEN CHILD was developed in productions at South Coast Repertory; The John F. Kennedy Center for the Performing Arts/Eisenhower Theater (James A. Johnson, Chairman; Lawrence J. Wilker, President); The Singapore Repertory Theatre (Tony Petito, Artistic Director); and the American Conservatory Theatre (Carey Perloff, Artistic Director; Heather Kitchen, Managing Director).

GOLDEN CHILD received its premiere at by The Joseph Papp Public Theater/New York Shakespeare Festival (George C. Wolfe, Producer) in New York City, on November 17, 1996. It was directed by James Lapine; the set design was by Tony

Straiges; the costume design was by Martin Pakledinaz; the lighting design was by Richard Nelson and David J. Lander; the sound design was by Dan Moses Schreier; the dramaturgs were Shirley Fishman and Jerry Patch; and the production stage manager was Buzz Cohen. The cast was as follows:

ANDREW KWONG/ENG TIENG-BIN .... Stan Egi
ENG AHN, daughter of Tieng-Bin and
     Siu-Young .... Julyana Soelistyo
ENG SIU-YOUNG, first wife .... Tsai Chin
ENG LUAN, second wife .... Jodi Long
ENG ELING, third wife .... Liana Pai
REVEREND BAINES, a missionary .... John Christopher Jones

GOLDEN CHILD was commissioned by South Coast Repertory (David Emmes, Producing Artistic Director; Martin Benson, Artistic Director) in Costa Mesa, California. It received its first workshop at Trinity Repertory Company in residence at the Breadloaf School of English, with assistance from the PEW/ TCG National Residency Program.

PLACE

Manhattan and Eng Tieng-Bin's home village near Amoy, in Southeast China.

TIME

ACT ONE: The present and winter 1918
ACT TWO: Spring 1919 and the present

GOLDEN CHILD

ACT ONE

Fade up on Ahn, a Chinese girl of ten who speaks in the voice of an eighty-five-year-old woman.

AHN.   Andrew — you must be born again. *(Lights up on Andrew Kwong, Asian, 50s, in bed beside Elizabeth — the same actress who will later play Eling. He sits up with a start, awakening her.)*

ELIZABETH.   What?

ANDREW.   Nothing.

AHN.   Make money, not important, write successful book, not important. Only one thing important: You love Jesus.

ANDREW.   *(To Ahn.)* Ma? Ma?

ELIZABETH.   Andrew, wake up.

ANDREW.   Sorry, I thought I heard ...

ELIZABETH.   Did you just say, "Ma?"

AHN.   Andrew — what this I hear, you no want baby?

ANDREW.   It's okay, go back to sleep. *(Elizabeth goes back to sleep. Ahn sits on the edge of the bed.)*

AHN.   Andrew.

ANDREW.   Shit! You're a Christian, Ma. Christians don't come back from the dead.

AHN.   You forget — I am *Chinese* Christian. Best of east, best of west.

ANDREW.   Yeah, worst of both worlds, don't remind me. What are you doing here, anyway?

AHN.   To become grandmother — why I must wait so long? Now I must help you ... so you not make terrible mistake.

ANDREW.   Ma, I've never wanted to become a father. This pregnancy — it happened by accident.

7

AHN. This may be last chance God give you, to make new life.

ANDREW. You were always hounding me: have children, go to church, follow Jesus' plan. I've never wanted anything to do with that sort of life.

AHN. You never go church, this your third wife. Already you prove you are big sinner. Now, baby — on the way, Andrew. Time to cast out demon of your anger. Time you hear my story again — not with ear only, but also with spirit.

ANDREW. Sorry, but that's the last thing I need right now.

AHN. No — is only thing you need.

ANDREW. To hear how you became a religious fanatic? No thanks, I think it's time for you to get back to heaven. *(Shakes Elizabeth.)* Elizabeth — *(Elizabeth sits up in bed. She's wearing ghost make-up and robes, and speaks in the voice of Eling, a Chinese woman in her early 20s.)*

ELING. The spirit of my unborn child cries out to be remembered. *(Luan, a woman in her 30s, appears U.)*

LUAN. Ah Ying! Tell the servants to begin the feast for Husband's arrival! *(Siu-Yong, a woman in her 40s, appears U.)*

SIU-YONG. Third Wife — you are responsible for seeing to it that the village is scrubbed and whitewashed. *(Ahn produces a Chinese man's robe from the early 20th century. Slips it onto Andrew, and he becomes Eng Tieng-Bin, his grandfather.)*

AHN. Remember? When you are little boy? You lie on my stomach, and I tell you story of our family. Winter of 1918. My father, Tieng-Bin, he make this family chosen by God. *(Pause.)* My father work in Philippine, make money. But like all oversea Chinese, he leave behind most important part of life — his three wife, his children — *(Ahn begins to speak in the voice of a ten-year-old girl.)* — all your future, Papa, you left behind in China. So after three years away, you got on a steamer ship, barreling across the South China Sea, towards our home village near the port of Amoy, in the province of Fukien.

SIU-YONG. Ahn! Ahn — where are you? *(Ahn exits with Andrew and Tieng-Bin. U., lights come up, revealing the home of Eng Tieng-Bin. C., the living room of the Main Hall, surrounded in a semi-circle by three pavilions, U.C., U.L., and U.R. Luan stands over a Servant.)*

LUAN. *(To Servant.)* What are you doing? Perhaps you don't wish to work in this house any longer? You would rather starve to death like your brothers and sisters, is that it? *(Eling enters.)*

ELING. No, Second Wife! He was only following my orders.

LUAN. You act as if I was going to beat him personally. You forget, Third Wife — some of us in this house were raised as ladies.

ELING. Maybe you should talk to First Wife about this.

LUAN. Who can wait for her? There're a hundred tasks I have to complete before Husband's return. And this waste of his mother's milk failed to carry out my orders!

ELING. First Wife said I could use him to whitewash the village.

LUAN. She didn't tell me. And what is First Wife doing — reassigning domestics? That sort of disorder only confuses their simple minds. *(Siu-Yong enters.)*

SIU-YONG. Second Wife, no one creates disorder like you.

LUAN and ELING. First Wife!

SIU-YONG. You can hear the bickering all the way across the compound. I don't care if you cut each other to ribbons, at least have the good taste to keep your voices down. What is the problem now?

ELING. She was about to punish — !

LUAN. He disobeyed my orders!

ELING. You said he could help me!

LUAN. I need all the staff I can get!

SIU-YONG. You two could give the goddess of mercy herself a headache. *(Ahn enters, as a ten-year-old girl. To Ahn.)* Ahn, go play with your brothers and sisters. Your aunties are making peace — which is never a pretty sight.

AHN. Second Auntie, are you causing trouble again?

SIU-YONG. You must respect your auntie as a true source of wisdom, I don't care how irritating she is. Now apologize to her, or I'll have you whipped. *(Pause.)* Did you hear me?

LUAN. She knows you won't whip her. You never whip her. No one whips anyone around here anymore. *(Luan crosses to Ahn, slaps her.)*

SIU-YONG. Now what are you doing?

LUAN. Just helping you honor tradition, First Wife.

SIU-YONG.   You have no right to strike my child! Only her nanny can do that! *(To Ahn.)* Ahn, go. And stop whimpering, you shouldn't give her the satisfaction. *(To Servant.)* Ah Ti! Go! *(Ahn and Servant exit.)* Listen — our Husband has been away three years and he will return to find his wives filled with love and cooperation — no matter how we feel about one another, is that clear?

LUAN.   I guess I'm just too honest for that. Hypocrisy sickens me.

SIU-YONG.   If you can't live with dishonesty, you have no business calling yourself a woman. Now — settle your dispute as true sisters. Or I may decide to find our Husband a fourth wife.

ELING.   Dearest Elder Sister, forgive me for my disrespect. I know I will never be able to match the great wisdom you have gained from having lived so many more years on this earth than me.

LUAN.   Thank you, Little Sister. Forgive *me.* When Husband made you his concubine, I took a solemn vow never to remind you of your peasant birth, or the fact that you were originally brought here to be my servant. I only pray that one day you will manage to bear him a child.

SIU-YONG.   That's what I like around here. True harmony. Now, everyone — back to work! *(The women exit separately. The pavilions are illuminated, revealing the three wives burning offerings to their parents. To her altar.)* Papa, Mama — on days like today, I feel like running away from all my obligations. Thank heaven for duty. Without it, we would be forced to think for ourselves. *(She burns ghost money.)* First, here's some money for you to wave in the faces of the other ghosts. Thank the heavens for inventing money — without it, what would we use to measure love? And here are more servants — in case you were forced to beat the last bunch to death. *(She pulls out an unrecognizable paper item.)* And — what have we here? Ahn made these herself.

AHN.   It's a steamer ship. Like the one Papa's riding on.

SIU-YONG.   Oh, Ahn.

AHN.   They want it. They want to be modern — like Papa.

SIU-YONG.   You think you know your father so well?

10

AHN.   From his letters. He likes modern things — not like you.

SIU-YONG.   The fact that something is new simply means it has not had time to disappoint us.

AHN.   Papa says, in the modern world — that they don't make girls wear bindings on their feet.

SIU-YONG.   Do you want to end up a lonely spinster? Now, listen. Your father spends his time abroad trading with monkeys and devils, he may come home with all sorts of new ideas. Don't be too easily impressed. *(She burns paper steamer ship.)* Papa, Mama, hear my prayer — let Husband return, if it is possible, a normal man.

LUAN.   *(To her altar.)* Papa, I forgive you for losing all our money, and even for selling me to be a Second Wife. All I ask in return is that Husband see myself and my son as we are: selfless, humble, and modest. And reward us with absolute power.

ELING.   *(To her altar; burning paper robes.)* Papa, Mama — here are the silk robes you never wore in life. With Husband away, life has been hard. But what's made it bearable is the chance to give you nice things. And, please, let Husband look at me with the same eyes as when he left. *(Crossfade down on ladies' pavilions, up on Tieng-Bin, who enters, kneels before the altar of his ancestors.)*

TIENG-BIN.   Papa, Mama, Ankong, Ama — I know I haven't been the most diligent son lately. *(He kowtows, burns paper money.)* But how can I explain — what it is like for me to work in the modern world — and then return here, to my home village, where everything remains as you and your fathers decided it should be? Can you possibly understand — you who lived your entire lives within the boundaries of this country hamlet, so far removed from any threat to your old ways? *(Pause.)* Then what do I do with my doubts? Questions concerning the very traditions you taught me? When I was young, Papa, you would order me to obey, and your strong hand put an end to all discussion. How much simpler life was in those days. *(He pulls out a small crucifix, displays it to the altar.)* I bought a souvenir for you from a Christian temple in the Philippines. A naked man nailed to some boards. They told me for good

11

luck, you can kiss its feet. They're very strange, the Westerners, and yet — hopeful, too. All the time talking about new inventions, new ideas. Nothing seems to excite them more than the future. *(Sound cue: music.)* Well, I must prepare for the banquet. Don't worry, I am still a good son. I go through all the motions, and curse myself for every deviation. In the house of his birth, a man is always a child. *(In the Main Hall, illuminated by half-light, Tieng-Bin and the ladies enact a stylized greeting ritual. They sit and begin to eat. Ahn rushes in from offstage, jumps into Tieng-Bin's lap. Lights up, music out.)* Hey, hey — who is this?

AHN. Who do you think? It's Ahn, remember? And you are my Papa.

SIU-YONG. Ahn — get back to your table.

TIENG-BIN. No, you couldn't be Ahn. You must be some impostor!

AHN. But I *am* Ahn. What's wrong with you?

SIU-YONG. *(To Ahn.)* Now!

TIENG-BIN. Ahn is just a baby. This person in my lap is a young lady.

AHN. Well ... if you won't believe me, then you're just ignorant.

TIENG-BIN. Oh, that mouth! You *must* be Ahn!

AHN. That's what I've been trying to —

LUAN. Dear Husband, would you like to see the rest of the children, now?

SIU-YONG. *(To Luan.)* No! We don't want her setting a bad example for the other children.

LUAN. It's a little late for that, don't you think?

TIENG-BIN. *(To Ahn.)* See the trouble you cause? Why can't you present yourself with your brothers and sisters?

AHN. Because I am a golden child. Kang told me so.

TIENG-BIN. Kang?

SIU-YONG. *(To Tieng-Bin.)* Her nanny's husband.

AHN. He took me gambling. Kang says he always loses, but with me beside him, he beat the whole table. So he told me I am a golden child.

TIENG-BIN. I need all the luck I can get. Perhaps I should take you back to the Philippines, huh?

12

AHN. Would that mean I could I take the bindings off my feet?

SIU-YONG. Ahn!

AHN. My feet hurt so bad at night — and they stink, too!

SIU-YONG. No one ever said that feminine beauty was pretty.

AHN. It's okay. I wouldn't mind. I *want* to end up a lonely spinster.

TIENG-BIN. None of my daughters are going to end up spinsters, understand? *(To Ahn.)* The world is changing. There's a whole new generation of men. Who will want an educated wife. Not some backwards girl hobbling around on rotting feet, filling the room with the stench of death! *(Silence; wives stare at Tieng-Bin.)* Ahn, go now. *(Ahn exits.)* First Wife — next time, I should greet the children before the banquet begins.

SIU-YONG. Of course. I hope our humble dinner meets with your satisfaction.

TIENG-BIN. Oh, yes. Yes! The ... roast pig, it gets better every time. When I'm in the Philippines, all I can think of is the way you make sticky rice in this village.

SIU-YONG. All credit must be given to Second Wife. The feast was her arrangement exclusively.

TIENG-BIN. Second Wife, you honor me with your gracious attention.

LUAN. Please, Husband. This is a task any child could've performed as well as I. But your son, Yung-Bin. He is such a brilliant young scholar, his tutor tells me he can barely keep up with him ...

SIU-YONG. Yes, we often see him chasing Yung-Bin across the courtyard.

LUAN. I cannot accept the suggestion that I possess even a shred of ability. The air itself is wasted on the likes of me. *(Tieng-Bin leads a toast to the smiling Luan.)*

TIENG-BIN. To Second Wife —

LUAN. Oh, stop — !

TIENG-BIN. — full of diligent support for your loving sisters.

LUAN. Stop talking about me ... This is more than I can take — to a woman of my upbringing, all this praise is sheer torture — *(Siu-Yong turns to Eling.)*

SIU-YONG. And did you see, dear Husband — ?

ELING. First Wife! Don't!

SIU-YONG. — the brilliance of our village?

TIENG-BIN. Why, of course. The streets, they nearly shine —

ELING. No, no — there're spots and stains all over —

TIENG-BIN. When I stepped off the boat, I said, "What? Is this the Forbidden City? Or America, where the streets are paved with gold?"

ELING. You're so kind to ignore my horrible —

SIU-YONG. *(To Eling.)* Shut your mouth! *(To Tieng-Bin.)* Some afternoons, I look out from my pavilion, and there she is, scrubbing the dung off the road as if she were still a peasant!

ELING. Once! Once, I saw some.

TIENG-BIN. To Third Wife —

ELING. So, I scooped it up, that's all.

TIENG-BIN. On every surface of this village, I see your goodness reflected. *(Tieng-Bin raises his cup. Eling points to Siu-Yong before they can drink.)*

ELING. No — First Wife!

TIENG-BIN. Please —

ELING. She deserves all the credit.

SIU-YONG. Third Wife! Take your praise bravely, no matter how painful it might be! *(They drink, then Tieng-Bin adds.)*

TIENG-BIN. To Eling — the sweetest and most fragrant flower. *(They drink again.)*

ELING. No, no, no, no — could you all please talk about someone else, now?

LUAN. Husband, Third Wife is correct to shine the light on First Wife. Without her leadership —

SIU-YONG. Hey, hey! Stop that!

LUAN. — this entire village would've rotted away and the first rain washed it out to sea.

SIU-YONG. What are you — retarded?

LUAN. First Wife — you said we must bear our praise bravely —

SIU-YONG. But you deserve yours.

LUAN. First Wife inspires us to work together, in the spirit of true sisterly affection.

14

SIU-YONG. Your mother should've drowned you before you learned to speak.

LUAN. To put aside petty feelings, and focus on our common goal. Truly, First Wife supplies the wisdom which holds together this sisterhood, this family, and this entire village.

SIU-YONG. Bitch. *(Tieng-Bin raises his glass towards Siu-Yong.)*

TIENG-BIN. I'm well aware of what you're saying about your older sister. In my absence, she is forced to be both Wife and Husband. To First Wife — who blesses this home with wisdom. *(They drink to Siu-Yong.)*

SIU-YONG. Why don't you pick up a knife and plunge it into my heart? *(They sit and resume eating.)* Nothing like a round of compliments to work up an appetite.

TIENG-BIN. I guess this is as good a time as any to share with you some of what I've been thinking lately.

SIU-YONG. Husband, we rely on you to bring home thoughts from the darkest corners of the world.

TIENG-BIN. On the boat, I met a man — an Englishman, a Christian missionary. We began talking — mostly, out of curiosity. After all, the founder of our Chinese republic, Dr. Sun Yat-Sen — he studied both Western medicine and Christianity. At any rate, this man — Reverend Baines — has come to run a mission here in Amoy. I've invited him over to continue our discussion. *(Pause.)* Don't worry — I don't intend to become a Christian. But it's important to learn about new ideas — following the example of Dr. Sun.

SIU-YONG. Perhaps, then, you will also study medicine as well?

TIENG-BIN. Well, I — maybe if I were younger, I ... that's a good one.

SIU-YONG. Funny the difference between Chinese and Occidental people. In China, we leave food at the altar for others. The white devils, they go to the altar and fill themselves with free bread and wine. *(Women laugh.)*

TIENG-BIN. No, that's not — that's a stereotype! I wish you wouldn't act so ignorant.

SIU-YONG. Forgive us, Honored Husband. We are just backward women — hobbling around on rotting feet. *(Pause.)*

TIENG-BIN.   Look ... what I said to Ahn — about the feet —
I certainly wasn't thinking about any of you.
SIU-YONG.   Oh no, of course not. The idea never even
occurred to us.
LUAN.   I don't even remember what you said to Ahn.
SIU-YONG.   Husband is too sensitive on our behalf.
LUAN.   I, for one, am very interested to hear what this Rev-
erend has to say. Perhaps I can join you sometime.
TIENG-BIN.   That's not necessary, Second Wife, I don't ex-
pect you to —
LUAN.   But I agree with you. I don't like the old ways.
TIENG-BIN.   If the Reverend comes, you're all welcome to
join us. But don't feel any pressure.
LUAN.   C'mon, Sisters! What've we got to lose?
SIU-YONG.   Second Wife, I am constantly amazed by your
rigid flexibility. *(Tieng-Bin claps his hands.)*
TIENG-BIN.   Now — a bit of the modern world for you each
to call your own. *(Servants enter, bearing three gifts covered with
cloth.)* Ah Ying! *(Servant lifts cloth off Siu-Yong's gift, revealing a
cuckoo clock.)*
SIU-YONG.   Oh, my — what a clever Occidental clock!
TIENG-BIN.   Here, let me ... *(He moves forward the minute hand,
causing the cuckoo to appear.)* The mechanical bird comes out
every hour. I thought it would be charming, hanging on your
wall.
SIU-YONG.   Yes, I'm sure it will do wonders for my insomnia.
TIENG-BIN.   Ah Tsun! *(He signals another servant, who carries a
gift to Luan.)*
LUAN.   Husband, you didn't forget me?
TIENG-BIN.   An ocean away, Second Wife, I found you impossible to forget. *(Servant removes cloth, revealing Luan's gift: a
waffle iron.)*
LUAN.   Oh! It's so ... shiny. What is it?
TIENG-BIN.   It's a waffle iron — it makes pastries that white
men eat for breakfast. I assumed — since you prepare the ban-
quets, that you would appreciate —
LUAN.   I do! In fact, it's so beautiful, I can hardly imagine
actually using it.

16

TIENG-BIN.   Good! And now — Ah Ti! *(Servant reveals Eling's gift: a phonograph player.)* This is perhaps the best the outside world has to offer. *(He slips on a 78 — a scratchy recording of La Traviata.*)* Western opera. A bit difficult to appreciate at first.

LUAN.   It's so ... primitive, so crude and barbaric. I like it!

TIENG-BIN.   This is called *La Traviata.* The story of two lovers who only wish to be together — but their society makes this impossible.

SIU-YONG.   I can see why.

TIENG-BIN.   Now — I've spent three years away from the children, I won't wait a second longer. Go! *(Ladies head for the wings.)*

LUAN.   *(To offstage.)* Ah Ying! Warn Yung-Bin we're coming! *(Luan and Siu-Yong exit. Tieng-Bin grabs Eling before she can exit, gives her a long kiss.)*

ELING.   Thank you.

TIENG-BIN.   For what?

ELING.   For answering my prayers. *(She exits after the other women. Lights crossfade onto Luan's pavilion. She is performing her toilette. Siu-Yong enters Luan's pavilion.)*

LUAN.   First Wife, aren't you supposed to be announced?

SIU-YONG.   For years, you've made fun of my policy against whipping. Well, strip off your robe and come to the courtyard.

LUAN.   You're growing soft.

SIU-YONG.   What are you talking about?

LUAN.   Even your threats don't have the usual conviction behind them.

SIU-YONG.   Tonight, at dinner — you went too far.

LUAN.   Really?

SIU-YONG.   I won't allow it.

LUAN.   Husband didn't seem to mind.

SIU-YONG.   It is the simplest thing to manipulate a man. Just call him your master, and he's your slave for life.

LUAN.   I, for one, trust my Husband's judgment.

SIU-YONG.   How could you? Inviting us to listen to the black

---

* See Special Note on Songs and Recordings on copyright page.

magic of some European witch doctor — putting us on the spot like that —

LUAN. I had to do something. *You* certainly weren't controlling the situation.

SIU-YONG. Me?

LUAN. You let Third Wife run wild! Far beyond her proper place at the table.

SIU-YONG. She hardly spoke a word all evening.

LUAN. Of course, I understand — the two of you have struck a bargain against me.

SIU-YONG. If there's one thing I try to be, it's fair-minded.

LUAN. And so you dishonored me at the table before our Husband —

SIU-YONG. I went to great lengths to praise you!

LUAN. — allowing Third Wife to go on forever, until he had to offer her two toasts instead of one!

SIU-YONG. So?

LUAN. One toast should've been more than enough for a slave, a concubine — but no, she went on, protesting, blushing, denying — that slut. Her modesty was absolutely shameless. And you just sat there!

SIU-YONG. I don't know why you keep track of such —

LUAN. Don't act stupid, sister. You, of all people, should know — humility is power.

SIU-YONG. You could've gotten toasted twice. Why didn't *you* keep protesting your unworthiness? Should I punish Third Wife because she showed a little initiative?

LUAN. I don't flaunt my submissiveness like some people.

SIU-YONG. You know what your problem is? Deep inside, you believe the flattery is true.

LUAN. And Third Wife is different?

SIU-YONG. She's not smart enough to conceal her real emotions.

LUAN. Then why is she the one sharing her bed with Husband on his first night home?

SIU-YONG. You can't possibly take that sort of thing personally!

LUAN. I won't be content with her soggy leftovers.

SIU-YONG. Husbands always go to the bed of the youngest wife. That's what they're for. To save the rest of us all that mess and fuss.

LUAN. Has it ever occurred to you, that our Husband is different?

SIU-YONG. And that's your excuse for putting us in this position?

LUAN. If Husband becomes a Christian, then everything changes. All roles around here are up for re-assignment. And the one who breaks the most rules wins.

SIU-YONG. Foreigners have been invading our country for centuries. We always change them more than they change us. It won't be any different this time.

LUAN. I'm trying to warn you, Older Sister, because I despise Third Wife even more than you. You — I find myself starting to pity.

SIU-YONG. What will it take to have some real peace in this house? *(Offstage, recording of* La Traviata.*)*

LUAN. Listen. They're playing that Italian opera. He brings her music, and me a gift for the cooks.

SIU-YONG. So? I've got a bird that tells the time whether I wish to know or not.

LUAN. If it's modern Husband wants, he's looking in the wrong pavilion. No one in this house will be more modern than me ever again. *(Pause. They listen to the music from the adjoining pavilion.)*

SIU-YONG. When you first came to this house, I watched Husband go to your bed and never complained. Why can't you do the same?

LUAN. When he started coming to my room, you took up the pipe.

SIU-YONG. So? I thought I'd finally earned the right to some real pleasure.

LUAN. I refuse to start taking drugs.

SIU-YONG. If you're determined to destroy yourself, there's nothing I can do to help you.

_____
* See Special Note on Songs and Recordings on copyright page.

LUAN. That's why you can't see what's going on under your nose.

SIU-YONG. Stay away from the preacher. If you try to show me up by becoming a Christian, I'll see to it that you're demoted to a common concubine.

LUAN. I'm not certain I can make any such promises, First Wife.

SIU-YONG. You don't understand — the pipe makes me stronger, not weaker. It takes away the only thing that stands in the way of a woman's power — our feelings. *(Siu-Yong exits. Luan looks towards Eling's pavilion, from where the music is coming.)*

LUAN. No, *you* don't understand. Right now, feeling is the only thing our Husband desires. *(Lights crossfade, down on Luan, up on Eling and Tieng-Bin in Eling's pavilion.)*

ELING. You shouldn't have praised me so much in front of the other wives. Second Wife will be fuming for weeks.

TIENG-BIN. But — just looking at you across the dinner table …

ELING. Are you going to make me blush again?

TIENG-BIN. I would never have believed my eyes could give me so much pleasure.

ELING. Just your eyes? What about your other senses?

TIENG-BIN. Well, you see, I thought I'd try out this new form of Western self-restraint.

ELING. What kind of ridiculous — ? *(She reaches for him. He pulls away.)*

TIENG-BIN. I'm restricting my intake of physical pleasures.

ELING. By now, your pleasure should be just about ready to explode.

TIENG-BIN. I've been living among the Christians, remember?

ELING. What does that have to do — ?

TIENG-BIN. They consider abstinence a great virtue.

ELING. Says who? I hear white men stuff money into their pockets and meat down their thick throats.

TIENG-BIN. Don't be so close-minded —

ELING. Oh? Am I not — what? — *modern* enough for you? You already insulted my feet tonight.

TIENG-BIN. I'm sorry. That was just a slip of the tongue.

ELING.   Where I come from, insults always get punished. *(Keeping her back to him, she crosses to the phonograph, sashaying seductively as she walks.)* So — you only want to watch? Like a good Christian? You say you are a modern man, who wants a modern wife? *(Eling removes her robe, revealing Western lingerie.)*
TIENG-BIN.   Where did you get that outfit?
ELING.   From the catalogue. I've been so busy improving myself. *(Pause.)* I like being modern, too. I like my new phonograph player. *(Begins to dance to the music, keeping her back to him.)* I like this *Traviata.* It fills me with feelings. Modern feelings. Delicious feelings of ... power. *(Tieng-Bin rises to his feet, starts towards her.)* No, no, no. Self-denial. Like a good Christian ...
TIENG-BIN.   Eling ...
ELING.   I'm your slave, remember? I can only obey your wishes. *(Eling eludes him.)*
TIENG-BIN.   What are you — ? You're going to kill me...!
ELING.   You must be able to hold out longer than that, Honored Husband.
TIENG-BIN.   I haven't touched a woman in three years!
ELING.   You expect me to believe that? The prostitutes in Manila must be for shit.
TIENG-BIN.   That's enough!
ELING.   My lord and master ... Sit!
TIENG-BIN.   Eling!
ELING.   Now, be modern. Sit! You wait for me to come to you. *(Pause.)* When you're away, I would put this on and imagine your face as you lowered the straps from my shoulders ...
TIENG-BIN.   Now, you don't have to imagine any longer ...
ELING.   Not yet. Will you please struggle for me a little longer?
TIENG-BIN.   But ... why?
ELING.   I don't know. It lets me know you care. That you suffer for me ... like I suffer for you.
TIENG-BIN.   Don't you believe that I want to spend every night here with you?
ELING.   Yes, but you have your duty to the other wives.
TIENG-BIN.   Eling ... you are the first woman I have ever been able to choose for myself ... and you will be the last.
ELING.   Now, if you like, you may touch me. *(He kisses her.)* You

know I'm going to pay for every one of these kisses.

TIENG-BIN. What are you — ?

ELING. When you're away, Second Wife bursts into my room whenever she feels like it, breaks —

TIENG-BIN. Eling, please. At least here, let's not talk about the others. I want to think only of you — as if you were my only wife.

ELING. That sounds so naughty.

TIENG-BIN. You're the one person from whom I want to have no secrets. This is my fantasy: that we will speak only words which are true.

ELING. Then can I tell you my secret? *(Pause.)* I like it. That you come to me — that you look at me different from the other wives ... I like it.

TIENG-BIN. Then look back at me. Don't avert your gaze, but look me straight in the eye. Watch me, watching you. *(They look into each other's eyes. Tieng-Bin and Eling fall into the bed, as lights crossfade up on Siu-Yong's pavilion. She blows smoke from her opium pipe at her family altar.)*

SIU-YONG. *(Smoking on pipe, to altar.)* Papa ... here's something special for you tonight. Mama — you too. A new blend made from Indian and Burmese poppies. It turns the worst insults of other wives into beautiful poetry. *(Pause.)* I know I've neglected you in the days since Husband's return. But can you blame me? I prayed for normal, and what walks into my home? A bloody pagan. *(Ahn appears in the doorway to Siu-Yong's pavilion.)* Here you are ... come, come. *(Ahn crosses slowly. Siu-Yong puts her pipe down, pulls Ahn down towards her.)* Daughter — you've stopped visiting me these past few nights.

AHN. I've been getting up early. To spend time with Papa.

SIU-YONG. You are a good daughter. Headstrong, but I'll tell you a secret — I like that. Later in years, when you grow breasts and hips, you will learn to appear obedient. But you will always remember a time when your tongue was unbound. *(Pause.)* I think it's wonderful, that you spend time with Papa. In fact, that's why I called you here tonight. I think you should see him even more often.

AHN. Really?

SIU-YONG.   Your Papa has invited a guest to visit, a white demon with skin the color of a day-old corpse. This man makes his living speaking nonsense.

AHN.   Like a clown?

SIU-YONG.   Only he doesn't know it. He is a clown who thinks he is a god. *(Pause.)* When this clown comes, Second Auntie will join them. To try and win your father to her side. I want you there, also — to tell me everything she does.

AHN.   When Papa's talking grown-up things, he always sends me away.

SIU-YONG.   Just pretend you, too, wish to learn some of this rubbish. Your father will be so impressed that his daughter wishes to become a "modern woman." *(Ahn backs away from the altar.)* Where are you going?

AHN.   I ... I don't want to lie to Papa.

SIU-YONG.   You refuse your own mother? And the ghosts of all your ancestors? They're already very angry with you.

AHN.   Why?

SIU-YONG.   Because you complained about your footbindings at the banquet.

AHN.   Do you think they like it when you smoke? I think you should stop.

SIU-YONG.   I smoke for strength to carry out their wishes. But you — you would rather Second Auntie take over this house.

AHN.   That's not true!

SIU-YONG.   All right. Then you are the one who must stop her.

AHN.   Why me?

SIU-YONG.   Because you are a Golden Child. You said so yourself, remember? Well, if you're any sort of Golden Child at all, you should be able to hear the voices of the dead.

AHN.   I don't know if I — Maybe I don't want to hear them.

SIU-YONG.   Ahn! To preserve the family is your first duty as a woman. If you fail, your children and grandchildren will abandon you in your old age, and when you die, your face will fade slowly from their memories, and your name will be forgotten.

AHN.   Wait. I ... I think I can hear them ...

SIU-YONG. Of course you can.

AHN. They're saying, they're saying ... "Don't be afraid ..."

SIU-YONG. That sounds about right.

AHN. They're saying, "We will help you ... make you brave ... so you can save your whole family."

SIU-YONG. Good. You see, you are a special child. You're my daughter. *(Lights crossfade, down on Siu-Yong's pavilion, up on Tieng-Bin's altar. He burns offerings.)*

TIENG-BIN. *(To altar.)* Papa, Mama — the servants found some flowers today, which had somehow blossomed in winter. I thought you might appreciate them. *(Lights crossfade, down on Siu-Yong's pavilion, up on Tieng-Bin's altar. Ghosts exit. He burns offerings, as Luan enters.)*

LUAN. Husband!

TIENG-BIN. Second Wife!

LUAN. Excuse me — I didn't know you were here.

TIENG-BIN. Second Wife, it's hard to believe anything in this house escapes your notice.

LUAN. Oh, you flatter me. Do you mind? *(She sits beside him.)*

TIENG-BIN. Actually, I was just —

LUAN. I usually come at dawn to tend your parents' altar. But last night, I couldn't sleep. Did you hear poor Ahn, crying in her room?

TIENG-BIN. Yes, I did.

LUAN. I understand First Wife recently tightened her foot-bindings.

TIENG-BIN. I thought as much.

LUAN. Husband, I am so grateful that you spoke out against footbinding at the banquet the other night. But I must tell you, afterward, First Wife came to my pavilion hysterical, railing against everything you said.

TIENG-BIN. I don't expect First Wife to agree with me.

LUAN. As for myself, the idea of having a daughter — with beautiful, gigantic feet — it excites me. Do you want that ... as much as I do?

TIENG-BIN. Actually, I do. To come home once more and see children — being turned into cripples — it makes me ashamed to be Chinese.

LUAN. I *knew* you would agree!

TIENG-BIN. Now, excuse me. *(Luan rises to leave; then.)*

LUAN. Husband. Perhaps you would honor me later tonight? *(Luan exits.)*

TIENG-BIN. *(To altar.)* Papa, Mama — Do I go to her? As obligation demands? Look at her — most men would jump at the opportunity. It's just that making love to Luan feels so much like doing business. Yet when it comes to footbinding, Second Wife seems more willing to change than I. *(He calls to a Servant, offstage.)* At Tsun! *(To altar.)* Why should we cling to a tradition that only passes down suffering, from one generation to the next? *(Servant enters. To Servant.)* Fetch First Wife. *(Servant exits. To altar.)* Every day I let pass without acting, only makes the damage worse. Oh, I can hear you — and all the ancestors — crying from beyond, "Some things cannot be changed." But don't I have the right to try? I accept all responsibility, assume all consequences. *(Siu-Yong enters.)*

SIU-YONG. Husband?

TIENG-BIN. It's an outdated, barbaric custom, and I won't allow it any longer.

SIU-YONG. What custom, Honored — ? *(Ahn enters separately, eavesdrops from a concealed location.)*

TIENG-BIN. From this day onward, footbinding is forbidden in this home, and the village beyond. I want you to remove Ahn's bindings.

SIU-YONG. One thing I have never doubted, Husband: that you are a good man.

TIENG-BIN. Let's not begin with the flattery.

SIU-YONG. Remove her bindings and you will rescue her from pain. Isn't that your thinking?

TIENG-BIN. Do you have a point to make?

SIU-YONG. Some pains are necessary in the life of a woman. In order to spare her a lifetime of loneliness.

TIENG-BIN. All that is changing! The new government has already outlawed the practice.

SIU-YONG. Tell me, Husband — would *you* marry a woman with unbound feet? *(Pause.)* For the sake of your daughter, answer truthfully. *(Pause.)* Men. You dream of changing the world when you cannot even change yourselves. *(Pause.)* Now — may I go while you consider the matter further? *(Siu-Yong starts to exit. Ahn reveals herself.)*

AHN.   Papa — I don't want to wear them. *(Pause.)*

TIENG-BIN.   Remove her bindings. Now!

SIU-YONG.   Once the foot is half-trained, to release it back to its natural state — her agony will be multiplied twofold.

TIENG-BIN.   If you won't obey, I will do it myself!

SIU-YONG.   At least allow us to be alone. *(Mother and daughter step into Siu-Yong's pavilion. Tieng-Bin remains in the courtyard. On the house speakers, ghost voices fade up.)*

GHOST VOICES.

> To betray your ancestors is to cut your own heart from your body.
>
> The undutiful son reaps a harvest of famine and ruin.
>
> Those who forsake the past enter the future without a tongue to speak or eyes to see.
>
> His children and his children's children will be cursed to the seventh generation.
>
> Only a fool turns his back on the wisdom of the ages.
>
> All things worth saying have already been spoken. All things worth knowing have already been made known.

SIU-YONG.   *(To Ahn.)* Daughter — you do not know what a terrible gift is freedom. *(Siu-Yong unwinds strips of cloth from Ahn's feet. In the courtyard, Tieng-Bin listens to Ahn's cries of pain.)*

TIENG-BIN.   *(To altar.)* Papa, Mama — forgive me. *(Lights crossfade. Music underscores the following: Luan, Eling, and Siu-Yong enter the courtyard to play mahjongg. A Servant brings in a calling card. Siu-Yong looks at it, women scatter to their respective pavilions. Reverend Baines, a white man in his 50s, enters. Separately, Andrew enters with Ahn, who is again his mother, an old woman.)*

AHN.   Andrew — when pastor come, this first time, ever I see my mother hide from any person. My father fight — bring change to our home. But when change come, come like fire. No one know — who will live, and who will be lost. *(Pause.)* This, first foreigner, ever I see. White demon! *(Fade to black.)*

END OF ACT ONE

26

ACT TWO

Special reveals Ahn, running and jumping towards the Main Hall. Area lights up on the Main Hall to reveal Tieng-Bin and Baines sitting over tea and pastries. Baines speaks brokenly with an English accent.

TIENG-BIN. Oolong.
BAINES. Oolong.
TIENG-BIN. Jasmine.
BAINES. Jasmine.
TIENG-BIN. Monkey-Pick.
BAINES. Monkey-Pick?
TIENG-BIN. Oolong and jasmine form the bulk of our export. But Monkey-Pick Tea is the pride of the province.
BAINES. Why you call — ?
TIENG-BIN. Because it's picked by monkeys, why else?
BAINES. I ... no understand.
TIENG-BIN. The leaf grows so high that only monkeys can reach it. So we train them to harvest the plant for us. Something like, among your people, I understand, there is a fungus that only pigs can dig up.
BAINES. Oh. Yes. Uh, uh — no can say in Chinese. But, not my people.
TIENG-BIN. No?
BAINES. No. I — English. Pigs — French.
TIENG-BIN. Oh, yes, yes. You're separated by a large channel of water.
BAINES. No large enough.
TIENG-BIN. We feel the same way about the Japanese. *(He toasts.)* To understanding.
BAINES. Understanding. Yes, yes. *(They drink.)* Oh, oh — very good. Mmmm. Yummy. England, we cannot drink such very good tea.

27

TIENG-BIN. Well, you lack properly trained monkeys.

BAINES. Mon — ? Oh, oh. Yes! I even learn — not to add the cream.

TIENG-BIN. Please! You might as well add cream to wine!

BAINES. Ha, ha! Tea such yummy, no need cream … and…? *(He points to the plate on the table.)*

TIENG-BIN. Dan tat.

BAINES. Dan tat.

TIENG-BIN. I had a special batch made up, in honor of your visit.

BAINES. Ahn, please — you come … also cake eat? *(Ahn crosses to Baines, takes a pastry.)*

TIENG-BIN. Ahn! What do you say to the Reverend?

BAINES. Please — not my house.

TIENG-BIN. You've been coming to visit us for many months.

BAINES. Not my cake.

TIENG-BIN. She must show you proper respect.

AHN. *(To Baines.)* Thank you. *(Then.)* "Yummy?" *(She pops it into her mouth.)*

BAINES. Yes. Yummy. Very yummy. *(He does the same. She resumes her position on the floor.)*

TIENG-BIN. I have to be honest with you, Reverend —

BAINES. Mmmm.

TIENG-BIN. I deal with a lot of white men in my business. Americans, Englishmen, Scots, Australians —

BAINES. No, no … Australians — we no think they white men.

TIENG-BIN. Well, we don't claim them as Asians, either.

BAINES. Again — understanding. *(They drink.)*

TIENG-BIN. Most of the white men I meet, we do business, but deep inside, I know they look down on me.

BAINES. Mmmm.

TIENG-BIN. And yet — when I listen to them talk, watch the way they deal with each other, I must admit — there's something about them I envy.

BAINES. Envy?

TIENG-BIN. Jealousy.

BAINES. Ah, yes.

TIENG-BIN. All of us are away from our families, Reverend. Do you understand what I am saying?

BAINES. Many ... temptation?

TIENG-BIN. Let's be frank. Chinese or Christian — men away from their families — are still men. Understand?

BAINES. Temptation. Men. Yes, I understand.

TIENG-BIN. But ... there's a difference between myself and the Westerners. They seem ... more able to forget, to pretend, even to fall in love with these other women, far from home. Whereas I — I can never forget ... that my life, my duty, lies here.

BAINES. You want forget? I think, Jesus no help you here.

TIENG-BIN. No, no, it's — how can I put this? It's not that I want to forget my family, quite the opposite. But to be Chinese — means to feel a whole web of obligation — obligation? — dating back 5,000 years. I am afraid of dishonoring my ancestors, even the ones dead for centuries. All the time, I feel ghosts — sitting on my back, whispering in my ear — keeping me from living life as I see fit.

BAINES. I understand. Christian belief: We are all — um, um — single person, is to say, all have own relation ...

TIENG-BIN. Yes, I've seen this and it's remarkable. I'll tell you, Reverend — I once listened to some white sailors talking to each other. One said, "I can lift two hundred pounds." Another said, "I have an education." A third said, "In my life, I have saved a fortune." I was amazed.

BAINES. They brag. Not so nice.

TIENG-BIN. No, in a way, wonderful. That they feel so free to say who they are, without worrying that they're making someone else in the group feel small by their boasting.

BAINES. I see. In mission school, where learn me Chinese — they make — um, um — invent — new Chinese word, for new idea. Word is: individual.

TIENG-BIN. "Individual?"

BAINES. Meaning, each man, stand alone, choose own life.

TIENG-BIN. Yes, those sailors were individuals. Speaking the truth in their hearts, even if everyone around them disagreed!

BAINES. OK. You try.

TIENG-BIN.   What — what are you — ?

BAINES.   Like sailor. You try. You also, brag yourself.

TIENG-BIN.   Reverend, c'mon. I mean, that sort of thing is interesting in theory, but —

BAINES.   I start: My family, own many land — in beautiful country, name of Wales.

TIENG-BIN.   Really? That's very impressive.

BAINES.   No, no! I brag, you also. I go seminary, top of class! Now, you. You!

TIENG-BIN.   I feel … OK, I run the largest Chinese-owned business in the Philippines. God, this is so —

BAINES.   Good, good. God tell me, "Baines — you special man. Help China!"

TIENG-BIN.   My peasants actually like me, because I try so hard to help them.

BAINES.   Beautiful!

TIENG-BIN.   This is incredibly self-indulgent.

BAINES.   You like?

TIENG-BIN.   Yes, I like.

BAINES.   I am good good cook. Yummy!

TIENG-BIN.   I employ good good cooks. Yummy! Yummy!

BAINES.   I have daughter, most beautiful, all of world.

TIENG-BIN.   One of my wives … is the most beautiful woman in the creation of any God. *(Pause.)* What a luxury. To speak the truth — in my own home, of all places. *(Luan enters, dressed in Western clothing.)*

LUAN.   Just say the word, and I will disappear!

TIENG-BIN.   Second Wife!

BAINES.   Mrs. Eng — Yummy!

LUAN.   You are too kind, Reverend. You spoil a Chinese woman.

TIENG-BIN.   You look so —

LUAN.   Atrocious —

TIENG-BIN.   — Exotic …

LUAN.   I mean, who do I think I am?

TIENG-BIN.   The mysterious Occidental.

BAINES.   Very modern.

LUAN.   I sent away for it about the time you started visiting us, Reverend.

BAINES. Me? Oh, oh...!

LUAN. You got us all very curious about Western ways.

TIENG-BIN. Did someone help you put that on?

LUAN. Yes, Cheng-Ming. Stupid girl. There're all sorts of strange support items —

BAINES. Oh?

LUAN. — for parts of the body that really should be able to support themselves.

BAINES. Please! Not for me hear, no, no!

LUAN. I'm sorry, was I being ... immodest?

TIENG-BIN. From behind, you could be a typical white demon — oh, excuse me, Reverend.

BAINES. White demon — me — white demon.

LUAN. But I could never be as graceful as those Western women. To get into those shoes — did you realize, they actually walk on their toes?

BAINES. Chinese woman — no can?

LUAN. *(To Baines.)* Well, you see, most of us lost our toes years ago ...

BAINES. Oh ... I see ...

LUAN. Maybe I could give my Western shoes to Ahn, for when she's older.

TIENG-BIN. Second Wife! What a generous thought. *(To Ahn.)* Ahn, what do you think of your auntie?

LUAN. I know what she'll say — I'm a freak.

BAINES. You look ... like Princess ...

LUAN. What do *you* think, Husband?

TIENG-BIN. I'm amazed that you can transform yourself ... into an entirely different person. *(Pause.)*

LUAN. Reverend, has Husband taken care of your tea?

BAINES. Oh, yes, yes ...

LUAN. And the dan tat?

BAINES. ... so much, I eat like cow ...

LUAN. You mean, pig?

BAINES. Huh?

LUAN. Pig ...

BAINES. Oh, yes, pig, pig — my Chinese ...

LUAN.   Your Chinese is excellent.

AHN.   Auntie, may I have the shoes? Although I do not deserve them.

LUAN.   *(To Baines.)* Listen to her. It's so encouraging to see even Ahn influenced by your example. *(To Ahn.)* Yes, you may have them. *(To Tieng-Bin.)* Your son, Yung-Bin, has asked for a Western suit.

AHN.   Can I see them — now?

LUAN.   *(To Baines.)* So Reverend, what lessons do you have for us today?

BAINES.   Oh! Well …

AHN.   I told the servants your story about the three wise men.

BAINES.   My — my — ? Ah, good!

TIENG-BIN.   Amazing, isn't it? That her mind is so unfettered by the past.

LUAN.   I am so fortunate Husband allows me to join you both. He is the most enlightened, most virtuous man in all of Fukien — no, in all of China.

TIENG-BIN.   You praise me too much.

LUAN.   Then let anyone in this house prove me wrong!

BAINES.   He is great man — great man …

LUAN.   This is what I like — honest talk! By thinking as he thinks — that's the Western way — the way of the future.

AHN.   Second Auntie —

LUAN.   The other wives, they don't feel so differently —

AHN.   Second Auntie —

LUAN.   Don't let the fact that they've never even said "hi" in eight months give you any other impression.

AHN.   Second Auntie!

LUAN.   What do you want!

AHN.   I want my shoes!

TIENG-BIN.   Ahn!

LUAN.   Husband, will you please tell this girl selfishness is unworthy of your home? *(To Baines.)* And it's not very Christian either, is it, Reverend?

BAINES.   My Chinese … very bad …

LUAN.   Well. I will forgo my lesson with the Reverend.

AHN.   *(To Luan.)* You said I could have them.

TIENG-BIN.   Luan, where are the shoes?

LUAN.   They're in my pavilion. Please allow me to —

TIENG-BIN.   No! I'll go. That way, you stay here, continue your lesson with the Reverend, and Ahn will get her shoes, too.

LUAN.   I really don't mind —

TIENG-BIN.   I'll settle this ... as always. *(To Ahn.)* Thank your auntie for her generous gift.

AHN.   Thank you, Second Auntie.

TIENG-BIN.   Excuse us, Reverend. *(Tieng-Bin exits.)*

AHN.   Precious Auntie, I'm sorry your feet are so dead and rotten. *(Ahn exits.)*

LUAN.   Do you have enough tea?

BAINES.   Oh, yes ... yes ...

LUAN.   Here, let me warm your cup —

BAINES.   Thank you, so kind —

LUAN.   You know, a traditional Chinese husband would never leave his wife alone with a strange man.

BAINES.   I ... strange?

LUAN.   The strangest. You're a foreigner. For me to be sitting here, pouring tea for you, by Chinese standards — it is absolutely indecent.

BAINES.   Ha, ha, ha ... I no understand. *(Luan offers a plate.)*

LUAN.   Waffle? *(Baines declines.)* He loves that daughter, favors her ... of course, he has no choice, she's so demanding.

BAINES.   Oh, Ahn! Yes, beautiful girl ...

LUAN.   Not by Chinese standards. It's her inner strength that impresses me. That she's managed to remain so brave with a mother who is an opium eater. *(Pause.)* Bean cake?

BAINES.   "Opium?" You say, opium? Drug? *(He mimes smoking a pipe.)*

LUAN.   Oh, no — I shouldn't have even opened my —

BAINES.   Ahn's mama? Opium? Mr. Eng, does he — ?

LUAN.   My only interest is in helping First Wife recover ... the drug makes her do things she doesn't mean — to plot against myself, my Husband ... you ...

BAINES.   Me? First Wife plot against *me?*

LUAN.   But if she were not a drug addict, I know — she would never force her daughter to spy against you!

BAINES. Please, slow. Ahn — is spy? How you know?

LUAN. The servants tell me everything.

BAINES. If this true. If Ahn is spy —

LUAN. No — no get excited.

BAINES. Must tell Mr. Eng!

LUAN. No — please, instead, kill me!

BAINES. "Kill you?" What in devil are you — ?

LUAN. Listen. If I tell Husband, he will not believe. Will become angry — at me, and you, also.

BAINES. So ... *no one* tell him? But —

LUAN. No. Someone will tell him.

BAINES. Who?

LUAN. Third Wife — I told her Ahn is spy. She says, "I don't want to hear!" But —- patience, one day, she will tell him ...

BAINES. How — how you — ?

LUAN. She will tell Husband because she wants to gain his favor.

BAINES. Why you tell me ... all this thing?

LUAN. Reverend — when Chinese men convert to Christianity, what becomes of their many wives?

BAINES. Best idea: Man choose, one woman be only true wife.

LUAN. And the rest of them?

BAINES. Can still live in house ... but like —- sisters, like —-

LUAN. And the Christian man should have a Christian wife, yes?

BAINES. Yes, yes —- this best thing.

LUAN. Well, then — will you be my advocate?

BAINES. "Advocate?"

LUAN. You understand. I think a lot more than you let on. I think we two can help each other —- once you see how I can be of use to you in your work.

BAINES. You ... help me?

LUAN. Husband says you have made few converts in many months. I can help you spread the word of Jesus, you see to it that I gain my rightful place.

BAINES. Yes?

LUAN. Reverend — the Chinese are a practical people. Let

me arrange a great feast — for the entire village — at which the Lord of the Great House pledges his allegiance to your God. You will be shocked how quickly the peasants rush to flatter my Husband by following in his footsteps. Like the Good Shepherd leading his flock. *(Pause.)* And one more thing: When you preach, never, ever say anything good about yourself — the less boastful you sound, the more you'll impress them. *(Pause.)* Oh! Your cup is cold. I am the most terrible hostess this side of Australia. *(Luan pours tea.)*

BAINES.   You ... you make Tieng-Bin ... to leave room, no? So you and me ... we talk, no? You make happen, no?

LUAN.   Don't be ridiculous, Reverend. This is China. *(Broken speech.)* I am nothing but woman and slave. *(Tieng-Bin enters with Ahn, the latter in too large high-heeled pumps.)* Oh — look at her!

AHN.   These are play shoes! They're too silly to wear in real life!

TIENG-BIN.   But you don't seem so eager to take them off, do you?

AHN.   They make me tall! — when I'm not falling over. Are you sure you do not want them, Auntie?

LUAN.   I have told you many times, I cannot wear them.

AHN.   Sorry. I forgot. *(Tieng-Bin crosses to Baines.)*

TIENG-BIN.   Forgive me, Reverend, for leaving you —

BAINES.   No — no —

TIENG-BIN.   But I have absolute confidence in the ability of Second Wife —

LUAN.   Oh, please —

TIENG-BIN.   —· to keep things interesting.

LUAN.   Our time together must have exposed me as a woman of very poor character. *(Pause.)* Isn't that so, Reverend? *(Pause.)*

BAINES.   Your wife — she teach me so much, way of your people.

LUAN.   The Reverend flatters me — he must have Chinese blood. The truth is, we had a very significant encounter. Now, if you will both excuse me. *(Luan exits. Ahn practices walking with the heels.)*

TIENG-BIN.   I settle more disputes here each day than at work during the height of the trading season. See how it is, Reverend? With such duties, how can I possibly feel like an individual?

BAINES.   Christian belief: each man, individual. But also, may I?

TIENG-BIN.   Please, please.

BAINES.   Prophet Paul say: Each individual man have only one individual wife.

TIENG-BIN.   Yes, I know that's the way of your people.

BAINES.   He say, your body — body of God. No join body of God with dirty thing.

TIENG-BIN.   Here in China, we say, whites are simply not man enough to handle more than one woman at a time.

BAINES.   What *you* think?

TIENG-BIN.   Reverend, there were times in Manila when I would see couples strolling arm in arm — thinking only of one another. And I would wonder ... what it would be like to live a simpler life. *(Pause.)* One wife? You whisper the idea as if it would offend me. When the truth is, Reverend, that it's a thought so precious, I whisper it too.

BAINES.   So, agree? One wife — who also love Jesus.

TIENG-BIN.   It's not that simple. You haven't the faintest notion —

BAINES.   This good, natural way of God.

TIENG-BIN.   No, it's wrong, it's shameful, it's the way of destruction.

BAINES.   Who say this?

TIENG-BIN.   The ghosts at the altar. "The righteous man holds his First Wife forever in highest honor." "The position of wives is fixed, like the bodies of the heavens."

BAINES.   This — evil voice.

TIENG-BIN.   My parents, my ancestors? Reverend, I couldn't even remove Ahn's footbindings without hearing their voices. How could I take only one wife?

BAINES.   Other missionary — they tell me about you.

TIENG-BIN.   What do you mean?

BAINES.   Tell me, Master Eng —· not like other lords. Others, when land fail, peasant starve, they shut their gate, correct?

TIENG-BIN.   It's none of my business what the other landowners —

BAINES.   Please. Brag yourself. *(Pause.)* You go Philippine, make money, save village. Other lords — they do this?

TIENG-BIN.   No, not usually.

BAINES.   Your own father — he do this?

TIENG-BIN.   My father always tried to do the best he could.

BAINES.   Before I come, already you not like other lords, not like father. Already you find new way. Must not fear to speak, truth you know in your soul. *(Tieng-Bin moves towards his family altar. Lights slowly dim.)*

TIENG-BIN.   I am an individual.

BAINES.   Good. Bible say, truth shall set you free.

TIENG-BIN.   And I live in a new time, much different from that of my fathers.

BAINES.   Yes, must be born again.

TIENG-BIN.   I should be able to make my own way, live my own life, choose the woman I love.

BAINES.   Prophet Paul say, "All I do mean nothing — If I no have love."

TIENG-BIN.   To act out of love ... to follow only the law of my own heart ...

BAINES.   Now, dead — no more power over you.

TIENG-BIN.   Yes. The dead are just earth and dust and bones. *(He kneels before the altar.)* Papa, Mama — you gave me life. But now I am a man. And you ... you are dead. *(Dim to two specials: one on Baines, the other on Ahn.)*

BAINES.   *(British accent, perfect English.)* "When I was a child, I spoke as a child, I thought as a child: but when I became a man, I put away childish things. For now we see as through a glass, darkly; but then shall we see face to face: and now abideth faith, hope, love, these three; but the greatest of these is love." *(Lights crossfade to Eling's pavilion. She lies in bed, nursing a swollen belly. Tieng-Bin enters, carrying a phonograph record.)*

TIENG-BIN.   Italy can never be ignored, but the future — it comes from America.

ELING.   What have you got there? *(He unwraps a new 78, slips it onto the phonograph.)*

TIENG-BIN.   This is a different kind of opera. Where men and

37

women dance together dreaming they are anyone they wish to be. *(He places the needle on the record. Scratchy recording of American dance music from the turn of the century.)* May I have this dance? *(He takes her hands.)* In the Philippines — I took lessons.

ELING.   You must've been even lonelier than I thought.

TIENG-BIN.   Come. I lead. You just follow. It's the way Western men show domination over their women. *(They dance together.)*

ELING.   I'll bet they didn't invent these steps for big fat pregnant cows with bound feet.

TIENG-BIN.   Eling — the few extra inches are very erotic.

ELING.   I'm swollen in places I never even knew existed. You wouldn't be like other lords, would you? And take a new ʿwife, one who's slim and beautiful?

TIENG-BIN.   Listen to the music. And try to imagine another world — better than this one. Where you ... are my only wife.

ELING.   You really held your teacher this close?

TIENG-BIN.   Eling ...

ELING.   All right. My only Husband, shall we — shall we take my child up to the hills for a picnic this week?

TIENG-BIN.   *Our* child. That sounds like an excellent idea.

ELING.   Like a peasant family, but with money. Afterwards, we can all come here, to the American opera house.

TIENG-BIN.   Except, our lives aren't only about our child. We're also two adults in love.

ELING.   That's why we got married in the first place, right?

TIENG-BIN.   And why we have no need — in fact, it would be impossible, illegal — for either of us to marry anyone else. *(Pause.)* Eling — I think we can actually live such a life.

ELING.   How? I think we would have to die, and be reborn as new people.

TIENG-BIN.   That's exactly right. Do you know what Pastor Baines and I have been discussing?

ELING.   I'm not sure I —

TIENG-BIN.   You. In a sense. He says I can pull down the family altars, live as though I had only one wife, even take you with me back to the Philippines. *(Eling pulls away from him.)* Don't you like the idea? Can't you see, it's the best thing for you?

ELING.   You want me to abandon my parents? Let their spirits wander alone for eternity? And if I went away with you, First Wife would lose such face. Is that what's best for us? To forget about others, and think only about ourselves?

TIENG-BIN.   I thought you wanted to be modern.

ELING.   I do. But does that mean I can no longer be Chinese? *(Record ends. Tieng-Bin removes the needle.)*

TIENG-BIN.   You know why this is so hard for you to understand? Because you've never even once attended Pastor Baines' lessons.

ELING.   You said I didn't have to.

TIENG-BIN.   But I — I thought you'd have *wanted* to come. Ahn took to the new teachings immediately.

ELING.   So I hear.

TIENG-BIN.   And Second Wife —

ELING.   Don't start telling me about Luan.

TIENG-BIN.   No, I really think even she's changing, becoming more generous —

ELING.   Husband, how can you believe...?

TIENG-BIN.   What? *(Pause.)* Eling?

ELING.   Luan runs around behind your back telling anyone who'll listen that Ahn is only pretending to be interested in your religion so she can spy for First Wife. *(Tieng-Bin stares at Eling.)*

TIENG-BIN.   Ahn ... has been lying to me? Ahn? First Wife put her up to this?

ELING.   I'm sorry, Husband, but you're the only one who believes in this new religion. For the rest of us, nothing has changed.

TIENG-BIN.   And you — you kept this hidden from me — for how long?

ELING.   I didn't know what to — ! It was none of my business. Second Wife should have told you herself.

TIENG-BIN.   This isn't about Luan. You shouldn't have left me in the dark. I'll get to the bottom of this —

ELING.   No! Please don't tell First Wife you heard this from me.

TIENG-BIN.   This way of life — it brings out the worst in us all. *(Tieng-Bin exits Eling's pavilion.)*

ELING.   Husband! Please! Don't! *(To altar.)* Papa, Mama — I only tried to tell the truth. *(Lights fade on Eling's pavilion, up on Siu-Yong's pavilion, revealing Ahn, preparing opium for her mother's pipe. Siu-Yong lies on the floor, in a drug-induced fog.)*

TIENG-BIN.   *(Offstage.)* First Wife — I am entering your pavilion! *(Siu-Yong rises unsteadily to her feet.)*

SIU-YONG.   *(To Ahn.)* Quickly — clear the air! *(Ahn scrambles to stash the drug paraphernalia, while Siu-Yong tries absurdly to blow the smoke clear. Tieng-Bin enters, causing Ahn to freeze in her tracks.)* Oh, Honored Husband. Please excuse the untidy state of my room. Had you given me proper notice, I would've had time to prepare refreshments.

TIENG-BIN.   Ahn — now — out!

AHN.   But …

TIENG-BIN.   Now! *(Ahn moves towards the door, trying to conceal the opium pipe.)* Ahn! *(Tieng-Bin snatches the pipe from her. Ahn exits from the pavilion, but remains crouched outside in the shadows, listening.)* Opium, First Wife?

SIU-YONG.   Really? Where?

TIENG-BIN.   How can you even ask? When I'm holding the pipe in my hand, the air smelling like shit?

SIU-YONG.   Not so hard. A good wife learns to disregard any number of facts. "See no evil, smell no evil."

TIENG-BIN.   How could I have been home all this time, and not even noticed?

SIU-YONG.   A husband is always the last to know. Servants are always the first, by the way.

TIENG-BIN.   Have you been sending Ahn to spy on my lessons with Pastor Baines?

SIU-YONG.   Who told you such a thing?

TIENG-BIN.   That's not important.

SIU-YONG.   How dare you — do you actually imagine I would ask our daughter to spy against her own father?

TIENG-BIN.   Why don't we call Ahn back? And put the question to her directly?

SIU-YONG.   On the other hand, it depends on your definition of a "spy."

TIENG-BIN. I see.

SIU-YONG. She was an innocent pawn, so don't stop thinking of her as your favorite child.

TIENG-BIN. This is my home! You're not going to undermine my authority. We're going to have honest-dealing here, is that clear?

SIU-YONG. What is this mania for "honesty?"

TIENG-BIN. Is everything a joke with you? Is nothing important?

SIU-YONG. Tieng-Bin! Don't leave me like this. We were promised to each other before we were born. *(Pause.)* What is family anyway, but a loose collection of people with nothing in common but blood? Does blood cause all people to think alike? To love, or even like, one another? Of course not! If we wandered wherever our emotions might take us, we would all have murdered each other ages ago. That is why, blood is not sufficient for order. Blood must be reinforced — by discipline. And your precious honesty is the mortal enemy of discipline. Confucius said, "In order to rule the nation, a man must first rule himself." So rule yourself! Tell me you haven't seen or heard anything tonight which would soil the honor of our family — and then have the discipline to believe your own words. *(She lays back on her pillows.)* Now — how about those refreshments?

TIENG-BIN. You are my wife!

SIU-YONG. And I'm trying to behave like one.

TIENG-BIN. This home is going to be a model of change! No matter what you or your damn parents say.

SIU-YONG. I have never stood in the way of change. But tell me, Honored Husband, how much change can people endure?

TIENG-BIN. And this life is better? You shoving poison into your body? Second Wife telling secrets behind your back?

SIU-YONG. Second Wife? *She* said I'd made Ahn a spy? And you believed her? *(Ahn exits the stage. To altar.)* Mama, Papa — do something.

TIENG-BIN. There you go again — worshipping your parents.

SIU-YONG. Yes, at least I pray to someone I know personally.

TIENG-BIN. Denounce them — or I'll force you to!

SIU-YONG.   No! Papa, Mama —

TIENG-BIN.   I said, stop it! *(Tieng-Bin throws Siu-Yong away from the altar.)*

SIU-YONG.   You — you order me around? Listen to yourself — scratch the surface, and you're still a traditional man, deep inside, you want a traditional wife, you want me to remain as I am, admit it! *(Tieng-Bin positions himself between Siu-Yong and the altar.)*

TIENG-BIN.   I'm so traditional. All right — have it your way. *(He grabs the picture of Siu-Yong's parents.)* What is it — that a traditional man does? Does he lose his temper? Does he order his wife around? Then punish her? Break her precious toys?

SIU-YONG.   No! Don't! *(He smashes the picture. Siu-Yong screams.)*

TIENG-BIN.   When she disobeys him? When she blows smoke in the faces of his children? Is this the sort of thing he does? *(He leaves the picture in a heap on the ground, stands back.)* I have made my decision. Or you've made it for me. I *will* be baptized. And all the family altars will come down at once. *(Pause.)* The servants will search for any more of the drug you may have hidden. Then — you'll start attending Pastor Baines' lessons. We all need a fresh start, to begin a new life. *(Siu-Yong remains on the floor. Tieng-Bin exits. Siu-Yong crawls to the rubble of her parents' portrait. She cradles it in her arms.)*

SIU-YONG. ,   *(To portrait.)* Papa, Mama — what terrible things did you do, that my life should go so wrong? *(As lights fade on Siu-Yong's pavilion, Luan opens her eyes, sees Ahn looking down on her. She is startled.)*

LUAN.   Huh? Ahn, you scared me! Idiot — have you added sleepwalking to your list of defects?

AHN.   I am a Golden Child.

LUAN.   "Golden Child, Golden Child."

AHN.   And for your schemes against First Wife, you must now eat bitter.

LUAN.   You know what Westerners say is golden? Silence. Now give me that lantern. *(Ahn snatches the lantern up before Luan can reach it.)*

AHN.   Your grandmother, I hear her voice. And she says: "Unworthy granddaughter, how dare you betray your sacred duties

42

to those who gave you life."

LUAN. This is the height of — *(Luan reaches for the lantern. Ahn slaps her face.)*

AHN. "Wicked Granddaughter —" *(Slaps her again.)* "You can't spit in the face of the dead, without eating the bitter fruit."

LUAN. Now give me that — *(Ahn pushes her down to the floor.)*

AHN. "How dare you strike your grandmother."

LUAN. You're ... not my ...

AHN. "Hear our voices, we starve, because you do not feed us."

LUAN. Ah-Ying!

AHN. "You scheme with the foreigners to turn our family against us."

LUAN. Isn't anyone on duty, here?

AHN. "As you abandoned your ancestors, so your children will abandon you after your death."

LUAN. Yung-Bin, Yung-Bin would never —

AHN. "Your son will grow ashamed of you, and future generations will not even remember your name."

LUAN. Yung-Bin will rule this family, I will live to see the day.

AHN. "No, your son will curse the day you told Husband that First Wife sent a spy against him —"

LUAN. What?

AHN. "For on that day, his fortune —"

LUAN. Wait one second. I didn't.

AHN. "His fortune was lost, his anchor-tether to the shore was —"

LUAN. If someone told Husband about your little assignment, it certainly wasn't me. *(Pause.)* What kind of ghosts get their facts wrong, huh?

AHN. You lie — you always lie.

LUAN. I'll tell you what kind — false ghosts. Who speak from the mouth of a peasant girl whose skin reeks of opium, who calls herself a Golden Child while, deep inside, even she knows she's an ugly little liar. *(She snatches the light away from Ahn.)* Ghosts have no more power over me. I'm a Christian now! So — would you like to hear *me* tell the future? I'm the only one

43

who's been right up to this point. *(Draws back to hit Ahn, ends up patting her on the cheek instead.)* Jesus saves. He will save me, and destroy your mother. He will take our miserable lives, all the injustice within these walls, and make everything born again. *(Pause.)* Thank you for letting me know what happened tonight. It won't be long now before I'm First Wife, in fact if not in name. Take my advice, Ahn — join us, forget your mother — and save yourself. Or else be washed away like the peasants in the flood. *(Ahn exits. Lights fade on Luan's pavilion. Baines enters and crosses to baptism font.)*

BAINES. Resident of city of Eng ... so good, see so many of you gather today, for great feast, wondrous fine festivity! One hundred thousand thanks to Lord of the Great House, Master Eng! Who give unworthy self great fortune, meet all you honorable friends. *(Pause.)* I — idiot man. My mother should have drown me in well before I learn to speak. Anyone say I smart, they no have brain. But Master Eng teach me so much, China way. Now, if any you visit ugly mission, hear my bad Chinese, I hope perhaps you find I am ... tiny little bit not so stupid. *(Pause.)* Now — wondrous miracle: Master Eng family — choose here, today — receive baptism, make holy water, swallow Jesus body fluid. *(Split scene: As Baines administers the sacrament of baptism, lights up on Siu-Yong in her pavilion with Ahn. Siu-Yong produces three balls of opium hidden in her altar.)*

BAINES. I call Eng Tieng-Bin. *(Tieng-Bin enters, in Western suit.)* "Eng Tieng-Bin, you desire, be baptized?"

TIENG-BIN. "I do, by the grace of God."

BAINES. "You renounce Satan?"

TIENG-BIN. "I renounce Satan and all the spiritual forces of wickedness that rebel against God."

BAINES. "You renounce sin?"

TIENG-BIN. "I renounce all sinful desires that draw me from the love of God."

BAINES. "Eng Tieng-Bin, you are seal by Holy Spirit baptism, mark as Christ's own, forever." *(Baines makes sign of the cross on Tieng-Bin's forehead and feeds him wafer and wine.)*

SIU-YONG. *(To Ahn.)* "The servants will search for your opium." So pathetic. Who does your father think the servants work for?

44

To hand me over to the missionary butchers — you must learn to put your foot down, Daughter. Such behavior is unacceptable, we mustn't allow it.

AHN. Mama ... don't eat that.

SIU-YONG. Duty calls. *(She puts the first ball into her mouth, swallows it.)*

BAINES. I call Eng Luan, receive the baptism. "Eng Luan, you desire, be baptized?"

LUAN. "I do, by the grace of God."

BAINES. "You renounce evil?"

LUAN. "I renounce the evil powers of this world which corrupt and destroy the creatures of God." *(Baines makes sign of cross on Luan's forehead and feeds her wafer and wine.)*

BAINES. "Eng Luan, you are seal by Holy Spirit baptism, mark as Christ's own, forever."

SIU-YONG. *(To Ahn.)* You will smile at the pastor, perhaps even kiss the Christian idol — but I know you will also worship and provide for me — in secret, where all the important things in this world happen. *(She eats the second ball of opium.)*

BAINES. I call Eng Eling, receive the baptism. "Eng Eling, you desire, be baptized?"

ELING. "I do."

BAINES. "You believe in Jesus Christ, accept him as Savior?"

ELING. "I do." *(Baines makes sign of cross on Eling's forehead and feeds her wafer and wine.)*

BAINES. "Eng Eling, you are seal by Holy Spirit baptism, mark as Christ's own, forever. Amen." *(Baines blesses them.)*

SIU-YONG. And you will succeed because you know the central lesson of life: that humility is power. And death is the ultimate humility. *(She eats the third ball.)*

BAINES. "We accept you into house of God. Amen."

BAINES, TIENG-BIN, LUAN and ELING. "Amen." *(Baines, Eling, Tieng-Bin, and Luan exit.)*

SIU-YONG. Now come here. And let me sing you to sleep. *(She takes Ahn in her arms, rocks them both while singing a lullaby.)*

> A BROTHER AND SISTER
> AS DROUGHT HIT FAR AND WIDE
> THEY SAW THEIR PARENTS STARVING

AS CROPS AROUND THEM DIED
THESE DUTIFUL SWEET CHILDREN
KNEW JUST WHAT TO DO
FROM PIECES OF THEIR OWN FLESH
MADE MOM AND DAD A STEW
TO SERVE YOUR PARENTS
IS LIFE'S MOST PRECIOUS GOAL
AND IF YOU'RE VERY LUCKY
THEY'LL ONE DAY EAT YOU WHOLE
WITH A HI DIDDLE DEE
THE SOUP GETS SISTER'S NOSE
AND A HO HO HO ...

(Siu-Yong loses consciousness.)

AHN. Ma? Ma? *(Ahn runs offstage. Fade to black. Lights up on Eling's pavilion. Christian hymns* on her phonograph. She kneels before her family altar, her parents' portrait replaced by a crucifix. Her belly is large in the final stages of pregnancy.)*

ELING. "The Lord is my shepherd, I shall not want." *(To altar.)* Papa, Mama — I have to do this for my Husband. He saved not only me, but all your children, from poverty and hunger. *(Pause.)* "He leadeth me beside the still waters ..." *(Pause.)* But if you see First Wife up there — *(Siu-Yong's voice is heard over the house speakers.)*

SIU-YONG'S VOICE. Three tips for a well-ordered household.

ELING. Tell her, please —

SIU-YONG'S VOICE. One: The less you know about your relatives, the easier it is to love them.

ELING. Don't be angry at me, I didn't mean to tell him —

SIU-YONG'S VOICE. Two: Never betray weakness in the home, it only encourages them.

ELING. I just couldn't let Husband fool himself like that.

SIU-YONG'S VOICE. And three: If, as happens in even the best families, a relative should cause your death —

ELING. Ask her to forgive me. As her sister? Bound by true affection?

SIU-YONG'S VOICE. — don't forget to return to take your

---

* See Special Note on Songs and Recordings on copyright page.

revenge. *(Siu-Yong bursts into Eling's pavilion. She wears ghost robes. Sound cue: Hymns crossfade to Chinese opera music. *)*

ELING.   Older sister! I —

SIU-YONG.   You learned your lessons in womanhood a little too well, I'm afraid.

ELING.   No, I didn't learn a thing. I'm a fool, simple-minded, an idiot —

SIU-YONG.   Quiet! You have some nerve, complimenting yourself at a time like this.

ELING.   But —

SIU-YONG.   Once, I actually believed you were stupid.

ELING.   But I am! I must be the stupidest wife in all China!

SIU-YONG.   Or the most clever. The other ghosts couldn't wait to reveal that it was you who betrayed me to Husband. It seems I grossly underestimated you.

ELING.   No, I'm a good person, a humble servant, a dutiful daughter —

SIU-YONG.   Dutiful — ? Oh, please.

ELING.   What do you know?

SIU-YONG.   You forget — I'm dead. I've seen your parents.

ELING.   No, you don't know them —

SIU-YONG.   Now that you have stopped providing for them —

ELING.   My brothers and sisters, they must be —

SIU-YONG.   What can they do but sell themselves as slaves?

ELING.   Slaves?

SIU-YONG.   Now they work for your former neighbors, the Wongs.

ELING.   Not the Wongs! The Wongs were evil people! What are they doing up there, they should be sent to hell!

SIU-YONG.   Maybe that's true, but *they* have dutiful children. How many times do I have to tell you: Life is not personal! *(Eling runs for the door.)*

ELING.   I'll call Pastor Baines — he'll send you away.

SIU-YONG.   With his Chinese? I wouldn't even be able to understand his exorcism. No, the only people who can protect you from a ghost are your ancestors.

---

* See Special Note on Songs and Recordings on copyright page.

ELING. I'll pray for them. I'll burn offerings, somehow …

SIU-YONG. What if Husband should find out? He'd be so disappointed. In his old-fashioned wife.

ELING. I have to be a modern person. Just like Husband. And Second Wife. And even Ahn.

SIU-YONG. Maybe *they* are. But you will never be. *(Pause.)* Some people were not created for change. Their minds are not large enough, their souls insufficiently ruthless. These are the people left behind, their names forgotten, as time rolls on. I should know. Look into my eyes — and see yourself. *(Eling falls to her knees before the crucifix and flings it aside. She lights the candle for burning offerings. Siu-Yong moves behind Eling.)*

ELING. *(To altar.)* Papa, Mama, I don't know what to do.

SIU-YONG. You know you're not fit to live in Husband's new world.

ELING. I can't let you starve, but I can't disobey my Husband either.

SIU-YONG. He'll take you to the Philippines, you won't know how to live there — with each passing day, he'll grow more ashamed of you.

ELING. No, I can't let that happen.

SIU-YONG. You are not the woman he thinks you are.

ELING. Maybe I'm not. But I love him.

SIU-YONG. Love! You don't know the meaning of love! You're grateful, that is all.

ELING. Sometimes, I wish I'd never even come to this house!

SIU-YONG. Then perhaps it is time for you to leave. *(Siu-Yong waves her ghost sleeves. Eling cries out as the pains of labor begin.)*

ELING. All these demands — how can I live up to them?

SIU-YONG. There is a way. To serve your parents, to serve your Husband.

ELING. How? Please, Older Sister — help me.

SIU-YONG. Come with me. You are needed elsewhere — with your parents. *(Siu-Yong shakes sleeves. Eling feels another contraction.)*

ELING. But … what about my baby?

SIU-YONG. Your old thinking will only spoil his future. *(Siu-Yong leads Eling to the bed.)*

ELING. Yes, I see you're right. It's time to prove … that I *can* sacrifice for others. This is the best thing for Husband.

SIU-YONG. It's best for your parents, it's best for your Husband, it's best for your child. And to a good Chinese woman, what else could possibly matter? (*Siu-Yong shakes sleeves. Eling screams in labor. Ahn enters, runs to Eling.*)

AHN. (*To offstage.*) Papa! (*Tieng-Bin, Baines, and Luan enter, ·cross to bed, D., of Eling. Hidden, Eling rolls off back of bed, crosses to Siu-Yong. Siu-Yong places ghost robe on Eling, leads her into the spirit world. Baines, Luan, and Ahn exit, leaving Tieng-Bin alone in Eling's pavilion.*)

TIENG-BIN. Eling? Eling. (*Tieng-Bin collapses at Eling's altar. He burns offerings with increasing speed and recklessness.*) How can I make you understand that I did it all for you? You must take everything now — everything with you — all my ideals, my memories of the world, my experience with far-off peoples — all the rooms I've filled to bursting with empty words — words of change, of progress — all the rooms where I had hidden our future. (*Eling's pavilion is catching on fire.*) Papa, Mama — is this is how you punish a disobedient son? Take from me the wife I love, even the wife I respect, leaving me with the one for whom I feel ... nothing. I don't give a damn any more about the living or the dead. Yes, by embracing the West, I have finally become ... an individual. (*Ahn enters.*)

AHN. All right, Papa. That's enough. Come out before you set the whole pavilion on fire.

TIENG-BIN. Ahn — this is none of your business. I can do whatever I want. Leave me alone!

AHN. "God will not test us beyond what we can bear."

TIENG-BIN. What kind of nonsense are you — ?

AHN. I listened to the words of the preacher, remember? Now, rise up and walk!

TIENG-BIN. You can't talk that way to me — you are only my daughter!

AHN. That is the old way. The Bible says ...

TIENG-BIN. I don't want to hear another word about this God.

AHN. "All things work together for good —"

TIENG-BIN. Get out!

AHN. "— for those that love the Lord."

TIENG-BIN. Shut your mouth! *(Tieng-Bin strikes Ahn, then pulls away, shocked. She stands her ground.)* Ahn —

AHN. Papa — You can hit me, but you can't make me go away. I'm not a little girl anymore.

TIENG-BIN. I should've listened to your mother.

AHN. No — she was wrong, Papa. *(Pause.)* Mama believed in our ancestors, she did everything for them. But when she called on them for help, there was nothing they could do. I watched her eat opium and die. So I'm not going to believe in them any more. I can't end up like her. I'm going to follow this new God, the one you brought into our home. Papa, we must all be born again.

TIENG-BIN. What have I done to you all? *(She leads him out of the pavilion.)*

AHN. You've thought enough for one life. It's time to let your children take over. So get up. The servants will be coming. I don't care how badly you feel, we don't try to kill ourselves in front of the help. *(Luan enters.)*

LUAN. Husband, such a tragedy! We must say a prayer for Eling and the child that was lost.

TIENG-BIN. Will you leave us, Second Wife?

LUAN. Oh, slip of the tongue —- my only Husband.

TIENG-BIN. Will you leave us alone ... my only Wife?

LUAN. Whatever you desire. *(To offstage.)* Ah Ying! Ah Ying! *(Luan exits.)*

TIENG-BIN. I don't know ... how to go on from here.

AHN. You must go back to the Philippines. If the business fails, who cares what god we worship?

TIENG-BIN. Daughter —- someday, when you are all grown, you will look back and hate me — for what I did to your mother.

AHN. Impossible, Papa. When my children ask about our family, I'll tell great stories about you —- how you made us all born again. But First Wife, I will not —- no, I swear, I will not even remember her name. *(Ahn begins to cry, collapses into Tieng-Bin's arms.)*

TIENG-BIN. Ahn, your mother was from another time, that's

all. I will always honor her name.

AHN. And I will always be grateful to you, Papa — even when I am old, even after I die.

TIENG-BIN. How can you possibly know such things?

AHN. Because I am a Golden Child. *(Lights and set transform. Tieng-Bin becomes Andrew, Ahn an old woman again.)* When season change, we leave forever, home of our ancestor. Your grandfather, after this, he does not live so long. Few years later, Second Wife send me far away, to new land, call "America."

ANDREW. You see? Why I don't want to become a parent? Your father tried so hard, but he only brought tragedy to himself and everyone around him.

AHN. No. He suffer to bring family into future. Where better life, I am able to live. I first girl in family go school, choose own husband — and all the time, worship Jesus.

ANDREW. So — whenever you opened a Bible, or said a prayer to Jesus, you were actually making an offering ... to your father. In spite of everything, you loved him so much.

AHN. My father, Tieng-Bin — this one thing I will never forget: You see, he is the one ... who take the binding from my feet. *(In bed, Elizabeth stirs. Andrew sees her.)*

ANDREW. Eling?

ELIZABETH. *(Waking.)* Who's Eling?

ANDREW. Sorry. I was just remembering a story my mother used to tell me. About my grandfather.

ELIZABETH. You never told me about your grandfather.

ANDREW. He wanted to start a new family with the woman he loved. And to make that happen, he tried to move heaven and earth.

AHN. Andrew — write it down.

ANDREW. You know, I think I'll write it down.

ELIZABETH. You never write about your family.

ANDREW. I want to preserve this. For our child. Like my mother did for me.

ELIZABETH. Maybe you should talk to your mother more often.

ANDREW. Maybe I will.

AHN. Next — you must buy nice house in suburb.

51

ELIZABETH. Andrew, I'm really looking forward to watching our baby grow up. And you, too. Now try and get some sleep. *(She kisses him, goes to sleep. As he speaks: Wives appear.)*
ANDREW. "I watch your mother sleeping, knowing you are growing inside her. And suddenly the room is filled with spirits — so many faces, looking down on me. And on each face, a story, some I have been told, some I can only imagine, and some I will never know at all. But many of them, people not so different from myself, who struggled with what to keep, and what to change — for the next generation. And I realize my face too will one day join this constellation. Perhaps, if I do my best, in the imagination of our descendants, this is how we are born again. I feel the eyes of our ancestors upon us, all awaiting together, the birth of you, my Golden Child." *(Elizabeth rolls over and holds him. First Wife, Second Wife, and Ahn sit on their bed. Lights fade to black.)*

CURTAIN

PROPERTY LIST

Chinese man's robe (AHN)
Ghost money (SIU-YONG)
Unrecognizable paper item (SIU-YONG)
Paper robes (ELING)
Paper money (TIENG-BIN)
Small crucifix (TIENG-BIN)
Cups (TIENG-BIN, SIU-YONG, LUAN, ELING)
3 gifts covered with cloth (SERVANTS):
    cuckoo clock
    waffle iron
    phonograph player and 78 record
Opium pipe (SIU-YONG)
Tea and pastries (BAINES, TIENG-BIN)
78 record (TIENG-BIN)
Opium (AHN)
Picture of Siu-Yong's parents (TIENG-BIN)
Lantern (AHN)
Wafer and wine (BAINES)
3 opium balls (SIU-YONG)

NEW PLAYS

★ **MONTHS ON END by Craig Pospisil.** In comic scenes, one for each month of the year, we follow the intertwined worlds of a circle of friends and family whose lives are poised between happiness and heartbreak. "...a triumph...these twelve vignettes all form crucial pieces in the eternal puzzle known as human relationships, an area in which the playwright displays an assured knowledge that spans deep sorrow to unbounded happiness." –*Ann Arbor News.* "...rings with emotional truth, humor...[an] endearing contemplation on love...entertaining and satisfying." –*Oakland Press.* [5M, 5W] ISBN: 0-8222-1892-5

★ **GOOD THING by Jessica Goldberg.** Brings us into the households of John and Nancy Roy, forty-something high-school guidance counselors whose marriage has been increasingly on the rocks and Dean and Mary, recent graduates struggling to make their way in life. "...a blend of gritty social drama, poetic humor and unsubtle existential contemplation..." –*Variety.* [3M, 3W] ISBN: 0-8222-1869-0

★ **THE DEAD EYE BOY by Angus MacLachlan.** Having fallen in love at their Narcotics Anonymous meeting, Billy and Shirley-Diane are striving to overcome the past together. But their relationship is complicated by the presence of Sorin, Shirley-Diane's fourteen-year-old son, a damaged reminder of her dark past. "...a grim, insightful portrait of an unmoored family..." –*NY Times.* "MacLachlan's play isn't for the squeamish, but then, tragic stories delivered at such an unrelenting fever pitch rarely are." –*Variety.* [1M, 1W, 1 boy] ISBN: 0-8222-1844-5

★ **[SIC] by Melissa James Gibson.** In adjacent apartments three young, ambitious neighbors come together to discuss, flirt, argue, share their dreams and plan their futures with unequal degrees of deep hopefulness and abject despair. "A work...concerned with the sound and power of language..." –*NY Times.* "...a wonderfully original take on urban friendship and the comedy of manners—a *Design for Living* for our times..." –*NY Observer.* [3M, 2W] ISBN: 0-8222-1872-0

★ **LOOKING FOR NORMAL by Jane Anderson.** Roy and Irma's twenty-five-year marriage is thrown into turmoil when Roy confesses that he is actually a woman trapped in a man's body, forcing the couple to wrestle with the meaning of their marriage and the delicate dynamics of family. "Jane Anderson's bittersweet transgender domestic comedy-drama ...is thoughtful and touching and full of wit and wisdom. A real audience pleaser." –*Hollywood Reporter.* [5M, 4W] ISBN: 0-8222-1857-7

★ **ENDPAPERS by Thomas McCormack.** The regal Joshua Maynard, the old and ailing head of a mid-sized, family-owned book-publishing house in New York City, must name a successor. One faction in the house backs a smart, "pragmatic" manager, the other faction a smart, "sensitive" editor and both factions fear what the other's man could do to this house— and to them. "If Kaufman and Hart had undertaken a comedy about the publishing business, they might have written *Endpapers*...a breathlessly fast, funny, and thoughtful comedy ...keeps you amused, guessing, and often surprised...profound in its empathy for the paradoxes of human nature." –*NY Magazine.* [7M, 4W] ISBN: 0-8222-1908-5

★ **THE PAVILION by Craig Wright.** By turns poetic and comic, romantic and philosophical, this play asks old lovers to face the consequences of difficult choices made long ago. "The script's greatest strength lies in the genuineness of its feeling." –*Houston Chronicle.* "Wright's perceptive, gently witty writing makes this familiar situation fresh and thoroughly involving." –*Philadelphia Inquirer.* [2M, 1W (flexible casting)] ISBN: 0-8222-1898-4

DRAMATISTS PLAY SERVICE, INC.
440 Park Avenue South, New York, NY 10016 212-683-8960 Fax 212-213-1539
postmaster@dramatists.com www.dramatists.com

NEW PLAYS

★ **BE AGGRESSIVE by Annie Weisman.** Vista Del Sol is paradise, sandy beaches, avocado-lined streets. But for seventeen-year-old cheerleader Laura, everything changes when her mother is killed in a car crash, and she embarks on a journey to the Spirit Institute of the South where she can learn "cheer" with Bible belt intensity. "…filled with lingual gymnastics…stylized rapid-fire dialogue…" –*Variety*. "…a new, exciting, and unique voice in the American theatre…" –*BackStage West*. [1M, 4W, extras] ISBN: 0-8222-1894-1

★ **FOUR by Christopher Shinn.** Four people struggle desperately to connect in this quiet, sophisticated, moving drama. "…smart, broken-hearted…Mr. Shinn has a precocious and forgiving sense of how power shifts in the game of sexual pursuit…He promises to be a playwright to reckon with…" –*NY Times*. "A voice emerges from an American place. It's got humor, sadness and a fresh and touching rhythm that tell of the loneliness and secrets of life…[a] poetic, haunting play." –*NY Post*. [3M, 1W] ISBN: 0-8222-1850-X

★ **WONDER OF THE WORLD by David Lindsay-Abaire.** A madcap picaresque involving Niagara Falls, a lonely tour-boat captain, a pair of bickering private detectives and a husband's dirty little secret. "Exceedingly whimsical and playfully wicked. Winning and genial. A top-drawer production." –*NY Times*. "Full frontal lunacy is on display. A most assuredly fresh and hilarious tragicomedy of marital discord run amok…absolutely hysterical…" –*Variety*. [3M, 4W (doubling)] ISBN: 0-8222-1863-1

★ **QED by Peter Parnell.** Nobel Prize-winning physicist and all-around genius Richard Feynman holds forth with captivating wit and wisdom in this fascinating biographical play that originally starred Alan Alda. "QED is a seductive mix of science, human affections, moral courage, and comic eccentricity. It reflects on, among other things, death, the absence of God, travel to an unexplored country, the pleasures of drumming, and the need to know and understand." –*NY Magazine*. "Its rhythms correspond to the way that people—even geniuses—approach and avoid highly emotional issues, and it portrays Feynman with affection and awe." –*The New Yorker*. [1M, 1W] ISBN: 0-8222-1924-7

★ **UNWRAP YOUR CANDY by Doug Wright.** Alternately chilling and hilarious, this deliciously macabre collection of four bedtime tales for adults is guaranteed to keep you awake for nights on end. "Engaging and intellectually satisfying…a treat to watch." –*NY Times*. "Fiendishly clever. Mordantly funny and chilling. Doug Wright teases, freezes and zaps us." –*Village Voice*. "Four bite-size plays that bite back." –*Variety*. [flexible casting] ISBN: 0-8222-1871-2

★ **FURTHER THAN THE FURTHEST THING by Zinnie Harris.** On a remote island in the middle of the Atlantic secrets are buried. When the outside world comes calling, the islanders find their world blown apart from the inside as well as beyond. "Harris winningly produces an intimate and poetic, as well as political, family saga." –*Independent (London)*. "Harris' enthralling adventure of a play marks a departure from stale, well-furrowed theatrical terrain." –*Evening Standard (London)*. [3M, 2W] ISBN: 0-8222-1874-7

★ **THE DESIGNATED MOURNER by Wallace Shawn.** The story of three people living in a country where what sort of books people like to read and how they choose to amuse themselves becomes both firmly personal and unexpectedly entangled with questions of survival. "This is a playwright who does not just tell you what it is like to be arrested at night by goons or to fall morally apart and become an aimless yet weirdly contented ghost yourself. He has the originality to make you feel it." –*Times (London)*. "A fascinating play with beautiful passages of writing…" –*Variety*. [2M, 1W] ISBN: 0-8222-1848-8

DRAMATISTS PLAY SERVICE, INC.
440 Park Avenue South, New York, NY 10016 212-683-8960 Fax 212-213-1539
postmaster@dramatists.com www.dramatists.com

NEW PLAYS

★ **SHEL'S SHORTS by Shel Silverstein.** Lauded poet, songwriter and author of children's books, the incomparable Shel Silverstein's short plays are deeply infused with the same wicked sense of humor that made him famous. "…[a] childlike honesty and twisted sense of humor." –*Boston Herald*. "…terse dialogue and an absurdity laced with a tang of dread give [*Shel's Shorts*] more than a trace of Samuel Beckett's comic existentialism." –*Boston Phoenix*. [flexible casting] ISBN: 0-8222-1897-6

★ **AN ADULT EVENING OF SHEL SILVERSTEIN by Shel Silverstein.** Welcome to the darkly comic world of Shel Silverstein, a world where nothing is as it seems and where the most innocent conversation can turn menacing in an instant. These ten imaginative plays vary widely in content, but the style is unmistakable. "…[*An Adult Evening*] shows off Silverstein's virtuosic gift for wordplay…[and] sends the audience out…with a clear appreciation of human nature as perverse and laughable." –*NY Times*. [flexible casting] ISBN: 0-8222-1873-9

★ **WHERE'S MY MONEY? by John Patrick Shanley.** A caustic and sardonic vivisection of the institution of marriage, laced with the author's inimitable razor-sharp wit. "…Shanley's gift for acid-laced one-liners and emotionally tumescent exchanges is certainly potent…" –*Variety*. "…lively, smart, occasionally scary and rich in reverse wisdom." –*NY Times*. [3M, 3W] ISBN: 0-8222-1865-8

★ **A FEW STOUT INDIVIDUALS by John Guare.** A wonderfully screwy comedy-drama that figures Ulysses S. Grant in the throes of writing his memoirs, surrounded by a cast of fantastical characters, including the Emperor and Empress of Japan, the opera star Adelina Patti and Mark Twain. "Guare's smarts, passion and creativity skyrocket to awesome heights…" –*Star Ledger*. "…precisely the kind of good new play that you might call an everyday miracle…every minute of it is fresh and newly alive…" –*Village Voice*. [10M, 3W] ISBN: 0-8222-1907-7

★ **BREATH, BOOM by Kia Corthron.** A look at fourteen years in the life of Prix, a Bronx native, from her ruthless girl-gang leadership at sixteen through her coming to maturity at thirty. "…vivid world, believable and eye-opening, a place worthy of a dramatic visit, where no one would want to live but many have to." –*NY Times*. "…rich with humor, terse vernacular strength and gritty detail…" –*Variety*. [1M, 9W] ISBN: 0-8222-1849-6

★ **THE LATE HENRY MOSS by Sam Shepard.** Two antagonistic brothers, Ray and Earl, are brought together after their father, Henry Moss, is found dead in his seedy New Mexico home in this classic Shepard tale. "…His singular gift has been for building mysteries out of the ordinary ingredients of American family life…" –*NY Times*. "…rich moments …Shepard finds gold." –*LA Times*. [7M, 1W] ISBN: 0-8222-1858-5

★ **THE CARPETBAGGER'S CHILDREN by Horton Foote.** One family's history spanning from the Civil War to WWII is recounted by three sisters in evocative, intertwining monologues. "…bittersweet music—[a] rhapsody of ambivalence…in its modest, garrulous way…theatrically daring." –*The New Yorker*. [3W] ISBN: 0-8222-1843-7

★ **THE NINA VARIATIONS by Steven Dietz.** In this funny, fierce and heartbreaking homage to *The Seagull*, Dietz puts Chekhov's star-crossed lovers in a room and doesn't let them out. "A perfect little jewel of a play…" –*Shepherdstown Chronicle*. "…a delightful revelation of a writer at play; and also an odd, haunting, moving theater piece of lingering beauty." –*Eastside Journal (Seattle)*. [1M, 1W (flexible casting)] ISBN: 0-8222-1891-7

DRAMATISTS PLAY SERVICE, INC.
440 Park Avenue South, New York, NY 10016 212-683-8960 Fax 212-213-1539
postmaster@dramatists.com www.dramatists.com